LIVING THINGS

ROBERT SNEDDEN

Fish

A⁺
Smart Apple Media

Published by Smart Apple Media
2140 Howard Drive West
North Mankato, MN 56003

Designed by Guy Callaby
Edited by Pip Morgan
Illustrations by Guy Callaby
Picture research by Su Alexander

Picture acknowledgements

Title page Solvin Zankl/Nature Picture Library; 3 Peter Scoones/Nature Picture Library;
4 Peter Scoones/Science Photo Library; 5t Jeff Rotman/Nature Picture Library, b David
Hall/Nature Picture Library; 6 Brandon Cole/Nature Picture Library; 7 CONTACT _Con-
3FE17F3164 \c \s \l Peter Scoones/Nature Picture Library; 8 Richard Herrmann/Oxford
Scientific Films; 9 Doug Perrine/Nature Picture Library; 11 Jane Burton/Nature Picture
Library; 12 Tom McHugh/Science Photo Library; 15t Georgette Douwma/Nature Picture
Library, b Dr Paddy Ryan; 16 Keoki Stender/Marinelifephotography.com; 17 Volker Steger/
Science Photo Library; 18 Solvin Zankl/Nature Picture Library; 19t Jeffrey L Rotman/Corbis,
b Galen Rowell/Corbis; 20 Martin H Smith/Nature Picture Library; 21 Doug Perrine/Nature
Picture Library; 22 Alan James/Nature Picture Library; 23t Jeffrey L Rotman/Corbis,
b Brandon Cole/Nature Picture Library; 24 Peter Scoones/Nature Picture Library; 25t Jeff
Rotman/Nature Picture Library, b Doug Perrine/Nature Picture Library; 26 Fabio Liverani/
Nature Picture Library; 27 Neil Bromhall/Oxford Scientific Films; 28 Solvin Zankl/Nature
Picture Library; 29 Dan Burton/Nature Picture Library:

Front cover Ivor Fulcher/Corbis

Printed in China

Library of Congress Cataloging-in-Publication Data

Snedden, Robert.
Fish / by Robert Snedden.
p. cm. — (Living things)
ISBN-13: 978-1-59920-077-4
1. Fishes—Juvenile literature. I. Title.

QL617.2S637 2007   7372
597—dc22   2006031886

First Edition

9 8 7 6 5 4 3 2 1

Contents

What is a fish?

What comes to mind when you think of a fish? One thought might be that fish live in water. You might think of streamlined creatures moving smoothly through the deep water of the ocean or of the bright and colorful fish that dart in the sunlit waters around coral reefs.

Some animals with fishy names aren't fish at all. A starfish isn't a fish and neither is a cuttlefish. Some animals such as dolphins and whales spend all their lives in water and look very similar to fish—but they aren't fish.

WOW!

The smallest fish in the world is called Paedocypris. It is less than 0.3 inches (8 mm) long and lives in peat swamps on the island of Sumatra, Indonesia. The biggest fish is the whale shark, which can reach more than 49 feet (15 m) in length.

BELOW *Coelacanths are probably the oldest type of fish in the sea. They were thought to have died out with the dinosaurs, so scientists were amazed when living fish were discovered off the coast of South Africa in 1938.*

LEFT *Whale sharks are the largest fish in the world, but they are harmless. They feed on tiny fish and plankton, which they strain from the water through their gills.*

BELOW *The ghost pipefish is one of the best camouflaged animals in the world. Can you see it?*

Extreme survival

There are fish that survive in the freezing cold waters around Antarctica, and there are fish that swim in desert spring waters that would be too hot to touch. Some live under water pressures that would crush a person, while others can live for a while with almost no water at all.

A huge variety

There are more than 29,000 different kinds of fish in the world. That's more than all of the amphibians, reptiles, birds, and mammals put together. Within this large group of animals there is, as you might imagine, a huge variety of shapes, sizes, and colors. Some hardly look like fish at all. Yet all fish have certain things in common that make them different from the other animals that live in the oceans, lakes, and rivers of the world. We will explore some of these differences in this book.

WOW!

The most common type of fish are called bristle mouths. They live in oceans all over the world at depths of 1,600 feet (488 m) or more.

Types of fish

Fish come in three main types—bony fish, jawless fish, and sharks and rays. Most fish are bony fish. They have skeletons made of bone, like those of birds, reptiles, and mammals. A waterproof coat of smooth scales covers their skin. Of all fish, 96 percent belong to this group, so most of this book will be about them. But first we'll look at the creatures that belong to the other four percent of the fish world.

RIGHT *The hagfish has a keen sense of smell to help it find food in the cold, dark depths of the Atlantic Ocean.*

Jawless fish

This group of fish includes lampreys and hagfish. As their name suggests, these fish do not have jaws. They have tube-like bodies and most are less than three feet (0.9 m) long.

Lampreys are a little like fish vampires, attaching themselves to other fish and feeding on their body fluids. Lampreys live in rivers and in coastal waters.

Hagfish live in cold ocean waters and are rather strange. They feed on dead and dying fish, and marine worms. They are slender, pinkish, and do not have a stomach. Hagfish produce huge quantities of slime if they are threatened. In fact, they can produce so much slime that a predator could be suffocated by it. Hagfish don't like being covered in slime, even their own. To get rid of it, the fish wipes itself clean by tying itself in a loose knot that it passes along its body.

Sharks and rays

Sharks and rays are more familiar. But a shark is certainly not jawless! Their skin is covered in rough scales. If you got close enough to stroke a shark it would feel like sandpaper.

Sharks and rays do not have skeletons made of bone. Like the jawless fish, their skeletons are made of a substance called cartilage. Cartilage is a tough and flexible material. You have some in your body, too. It covers the ends of your bones and allows your joints to move smoothly.

Most sharks and rays are excellent swimmers and live by catching and eating other animals. Sharks are especially streamlined and built for nonstop swimming throughout the open ocean. Rays have flat bodies and large, wing-like fins that make them look like an alien spacecraft cruising through the water. Many rays spend a lot of their time feeding on the sea floor and are cleverly camouflaged.

ABOVE *The torpedo ray is one of several types of electric rays that live all over the world. They stun their prey with an electric shock.*

Moving underwater

Have you ever tried swimming underwater? It is hard work and difficult to go very fast. Yet fish seem to manage it with ease, speeding through the water and effortlessly changing direction. How do they do it?

Slime and streamlining

Most fish have a streamlined shape to help them move through the water with minimum resistance. A fish's skin also produces a sort of slime, or mucus, that makes the water flow smoothly past it. Fish slime isn't just good for streamlining, it also protects the fish from parasites and infection. Some fish produce a poisonous slime that discourages other animals from eating them.

The streamlined body of the blue-finned tunny allows it to move smoothly through the water.

LEFT *Coral reef fish can make sudden changes in direction to escape capture— these are fairy basslets.*

Swim bladder

Most bony fish have a gas-filled bag called a swim bladder inside them. The swim bladder changes the fish's buoyancy and allows the fish to go up and down in the water. If the fish lets more gas into its swim bladder, it rises. If it lets gas out, it sinks.

Sharks don't have swim bladders. People once thought that they had to keep swimming all the time to avoid sinking to the bottom. In fact, sharks have a very large oily liver. Oil is lighter than water and helps to keep sharks from sinking.

Muscle power

The muscles of a fish help it move in any direction. Up to four-fifths of some fish is muscle, which is what makes fish so good to eat. If they need to move quickly, fish use the big muscles along their sides. These bend the fish from side to side in a slight S-shape. The power to move forward comes from the fish's tail, which pushes against the water. Some fish keep their bodies more or less still and move only their tails.

Cruisers and bursters

Fish swim in different ways according to their different lifestyles. Fish such as salmon and tuna are always on the move. Cruising through the water, they can cover long distances very quickly. The blue-finned tunny, which is a type of tuna, is probably the fastest fish in the sea over long distances. It can swim more than 37 miles (60 km) per hour.

Many fish stay more or less in the same place, such as in a seaweed bed or a coral reef. These fish are highly maneuverable, relying on swift changes of direction and sudden bursts of speed to catch a meal or to escape being eaten themselves.

WOW!

The champion sprinter of the ocean is the cosmopolitan sailfish. One was measured traveling at a speed of 68 miles (109 km) per hour. That's faster than a cheetah, which can reach a speed of 62 miles (100 km) per hour. The slowest mover is the seahorse, which moves along at around 66 feet (20 m) per hour.

Fins

All fish have fins. A fish uses its fins to steer through the water, to keep its balance, and to adjust its speed or stop. Some fish have fins for decoration or for protection.

Paired fins

Some fins come in pairs, like arms and legs. There are two kinds of paired fins: pectoral fins on either side of the body, just behind the head, and pelvic fins, which are usually on the underside behind the pectorals. Big, ocean-going fish have pectoral fins that are horizontal—these keep the fish stable and prevent it from rolling as it swims. Other fish, such as reef fish that need to change direction quickly, have pectoral fins that are nearly vertical. These act like brakes, allowing the fish to make sharp turns.

FINS OF A FISH

This diagram shows where the fins are positioned on a typical fish.

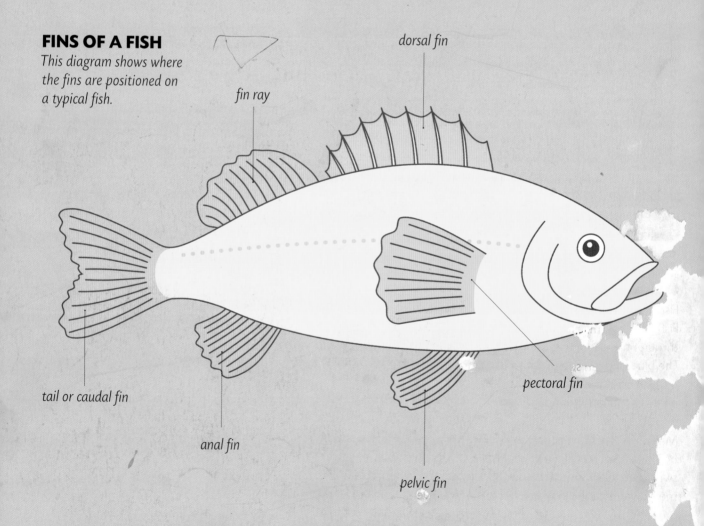

fin ray

dorsal fin

tail or caudal fin

anal fin

pelvic fin

pectoral fin

Central fins

A fish has a dorsal fin along its back and an anal fin on its belly. The main job of these two fins is to stop the fish from rolling over in the water. The job of the caudal fin on the tail is to propel the fish through water. A few fish, such as seahorses and sunfish, do not have strong caudal fins. The seahorse uses its pectoral and pelvic fins to move through the water, while the sunfish waves its long anal and dorsal fins as it swims.

LEFT *Mudskippers can leave the water and move across land with their fins for a short time.*

Flying fins

Some fish use their fins to briefly fly. Flying fish and flying gurnards have large pectoral fins that can be used like wings. As they swim at more than 18 miles (29 km) per hour, these fish can leap out of the water and glide using their outstretched pectorals. A flight can last for as long as ten seconds, often long enough to evade a predator in the water below.

Foot fins

Some fish use their fins like legs. Tripod fish stand on the bottom of the sea supported by their pelvic and caudal fins. Mudskippers can leave the water for a short time to look for food on muddy shores. They use their pectoral and pelvic fins to move around on land.

WOW!

Part of the dorsal fin of the deep-sea angler fish can be stretched out to form a kind of fishing line. The angler uses it to attract fish it plans to eat. The long fin glows at the end, and the angler fish flicks it out like a fisherman casting his line.

Breathing underwater

All animals need oxygen to survive because it helps them get energy from the food they eat. Land animals get the oxygen they need by breathing the air around them. How do fish manage to get the oxygen they need while underwater?

Dissolved oxygen

Water contains some oxygen in the form of tiny bubbles of gas that are too small to see. This is called dissolved oxygen. There isn't very much of it, less than one-twentieth of the oxygen in the air. The amount can vary according to different conditions—for instance, the colder the water, the more oxygen it can hold.

Lungfish live in places where there is a long dry season each year. They survive in burrows, breathing air until it rains again.

Gills

Fish take oxygen from the water through their gills. All fish have a pair of gills, one on each side of the head. Gills do the same job as lungs but they are adapted to work underwater. The gills are very delicate and are protected by a hard gill flap.

When a fish opens and closes its mouth, it is pumping water over its gills. Each gill has rows of filaments that are folded many times to create a large area for absorbing oxygen from the water. The gills contain many tiny blood vessels, and the oxygen passes into these vessels. The oxygen is then carried by the bloodstream, which delivers it to the cells in the body. Once the water has passed over the gills, the gill flap opens to let the water back out.

Lungfish

A fish needs to keep water flowing over its gills. If it is taken out of the water, the many, thin folds of the gills collapse and the fish suffocates. However, some fish—for example, lungfish that live in Africa and South America—can breathe out of water for a while. They don't have lungs, but they have a specialized swim bladder that can absorb oxygen, allowing them to survive if the water where they live dries up. The lungfish burrows into the mud and breathes through its swim bladder, keeping its gills closed until the rain comes again.

WOW!

If you could take a fish's gills and flatten them into a single sheet, they would cover an area 10 times bigger than the fish's body.

HOW WATER FLOWS OVER THE GILLS

Water flows in through the fish's mouth and over its gills, which absorb oxygen. Then the gill flaps open and the water flows out.

water flows into fish's mouth

eye

gill rakers

gill filament

water out

water out

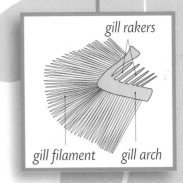

gill rakers

gill filament   gill arch

Seeing underwater

The eyes of a fish have some similarities to those of many other animals, including humans. But there are also differences, which help fish see better underwater.

Keeping in focus

The part of your eye that brings what you see into focus is called the lens. It bends the light that passes through it onto the sensitive, light-collecting part of the eye called the retina. It works well for light traveling through air, but the lens doesn't bend the light enough when it is traveling to your eye through water. This is why things look blurry when you swim underwater.

HOW A FISH EYE COMPARES WITH A HUMAN EYE

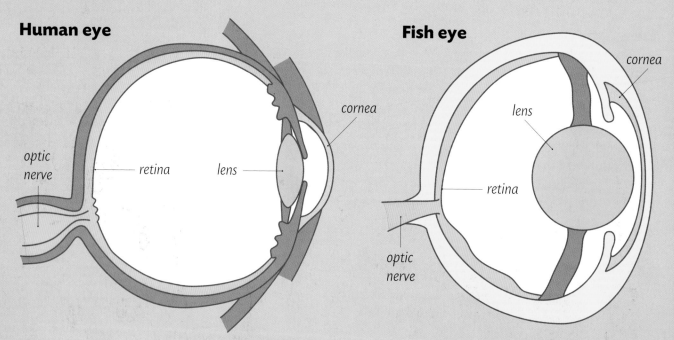

Human eye

optic nerve

retina

lens

cornea

Fish eye

cornea

lens

retina

optic nerve

The lens in your eye is oval-shaped. The lens in a fish's eye is almost perfectly round—this is why fish look pop-eyed. The spherical, or round, shape of the fish's lens bends the light passing through it much more than your oval lens, so fish eyes work much better underwater than human eyes. Human eyes adjust focus by changing the shape of the lens, but a fish's lens actually moves backward and forward to change focus, just like a camera lens does.

RIGHT *A crocodile fish lies on the sea floor, waiting for a meal. This one is in the Red Sea.*

Gathering light

Light doesn't travel far through water. The deeper the water, the darker it is. Fish that live in deep water have large eyes that are very sensitive to light. They may be the most sensitive eyes of any animal.

Deep in the ocean, there is no light at all. The fish in the deepest parts of the ocean have very small eyes. They may only see occasional flashes of light, and they can't make out shapes. Around 90 percent of the fish and other animals that live deep in the ocean can make their own light. Sea dragons and other fish attract their prey with a glowing light called a lure.

Four-eyed fish

Fish called anableps (the name means "looking upward") live in the rivers of Central and South America. They have unusual eyes that are adapted to see both in and out of the water. They can even do both at the same time. Their eyes are divided into upper and lower halves. The top half is suited for seeing in the air and the bottom half for seeing underwater. This allows the fish to watch for insects skimming the surface of the water, but also to spot anything coming from below to eat it!

LEFT *This anableps floats just beneath the surface of the water, keeping an eye on things above and below at the same time.*

Hearing underwater

Sound travels well in water. It actually travels faster through water than through air. But if you swim underwater you've probably noticed that the sounds are different than on land. That's because our ears, which are normally so good at hearing, just don't work the same way underwater.

Eardrums and capsules

We have an eardrum inside both our ears. These are like very thin skins that vibrate when sound enters the ear. This vibration is passed to another part of the ear—the eardrum—where the sounds are heard. However, our eardrums don't vibrate well when our ears are full of water.

Fish don't have eardrums. In fact, the ears of most fish aren't open to the outside at all. They are just behind the fish's eyes, protected inside capsules on either side of its head. Sound waves travel through the fish's body to its ears. When you are underwater, sound travels through your head, too. This is another reason why the sounds seem different underwater.

The cusk eel makes a drumming sound by beating on its swim bladder with a special backbone. It lives along the coasts of North America.

Swim bladder hearing

Many types of fish detect sound with their swim bladders. The walls of the swim bladder act like eardrums and are made to vibrate by sounds passing through the water. The vibrations of the swim bladder are passed along to the fish's ears, usually by a chain of tiny bones. Some fish have tubes rather than bones that link their swim bladder to their ear capsules.

Fish sounds

Sounds are important to a fish. Fish make powerful calls to each other that can travel for several miles through the water. Some fish make noises by grinding their teeth together, others by rubbing their fins against their bodies. There are fish with special drumming muscles, which they use to make sounds with their swim bladders. Many fish are very noisy eaters. Often, fish are attracted to the sound of another fish feeding, and they come to see if there is any food for them, too.

WOW!

The male oyster toadfish makes a sound like a ship's foghorn by rapidly contracting its swim bladder at a rate of 200 times per second. It does this to attract a female.

BELOW *Oyster toadfish live in the coastal waters of eastern North America and eat other fish, crustaceans, and mollusks.*

Tastes and smells

We taste things with the taste buds on our tongues. A fish has taste buds not only on its tongue, but also all over its mouth, on its lips, and on other parts of its body, too.

Some fish, such as catfish and cod, have long feelers called barbels around their mouths. Taste buds on these barbels help the catfish detect food on the bottom of a muddy river and help cod find food at the bottom of the sea.

BELOW *A shoal of striped catfish searches for food in the sand using sensitive barbels.*

Fish smells

Many fish have nostrils on their heads. Like us, they use their nostrils to detect smells, but they don't use them for breathing. Some fish use smells to alert other fish to danger. If the skin of a minnow is broken, perhaps because it has been bitten, it produces a substance that warns. Other minnows swimming nearby move away from the danger.

Swimming noses

Sharks have an incredible sense of smell. They have been described as "swimming noses." Around two-thirds of a shark's brain may be involved in smelling. A shark can detect the equivalent of one drop of blood in a swimming pool. It can even tell the direction the smell is coming from.

ABOVE *The gray nurse shark is not as dangerous as it looks. It will sniff out fish, squid, crabs, and lobster, but will only attack humans if it is threatened.*

BELOW *Pacific salmon heading upstream to spawn attempt to leap up the waterfalls of the Brooks River in Alaska's Katmai National Park.*

The smell of home

When salmon become adults, they leave the river where they were born and swim out to the ocean. Young salmon from many rivers form schools together. When the time comes for them to lay their eggs, the adult salmon swim back to their home river. No one is sure how they manage to do this but one possibility is that they find the right place by remembering how it smelled and tasted.

WOW!

The Atlantic salmon's sense of smell is a thousand times more sensitive than that of a dog. It is so sensitive that a solution of one part human skin in 80 billion parts water stopped a salmon from going upstream for half an hour after it was put in a river.

Fish senses

As well as having senses of hearing, sight, taste, and smell just as we have, fish have some special senses that are all their own. One of these is similar to our sense of touch.

BELOW *These roaches each have a lateral line that runs from just behind the gills to the tail.*

Lateral lines

If you look carefully at the side of a fish, you will see a line running the length of its body. This is called the lateral line. It is made up of a row of sensitive detectors that can pick up changes in the water pressure around the fish. Some amphibians that spend a lot of time in the water have lateral lines, too.

Tiny pores, or pits, in the skin are open to the water, along the lateral line. At the bottom of these pores, there is a line of tiny canals filled with water. Fine hairs along the canals detect the slightest movement of the water. The fish uses this information to tell which direction a disturbance is coming from.

Fish that live in schools, or shoals, use their lateral line detectors to avoid colliding with each other. If a shoal is disturbed by a predator, the fish will hurry off through the water at great speed, but they will never collide with each other.

Look out!

Lateral line detectors are one of the reasons you almost never see a fish bump into the glass wall of a fish tank. Detectors on the fish's head can feel the change in pressure caused by the water pushing against something. This tells the fish that there is an obstacle nearby.

BELOW *The Pacific Ocean hammerhead shark has sensitive detectors in its head that can pick up tiny electric currents in the water.*

Electric senses

The muscles of all animals produce tiny bursts of electricity when they work. Some fish, especially sharks and dogfish, can detect this electricity. A dogfish can find a flounder buried in the sand on the seabed by sensing the electricity coming from the other fish. A hammerhead shark searching for a meal sweeps its head from side to side, like a person with a metal detector, to find fish hidden in the sand at the bottom of the sea.

Electric eels and some other fish have special muscles that can produce strong pulses of electricity all at once. The charge is powerful enough to stun other animals, which is useful for defense and for catching prey. Electric eels also use smaller charges to find their way though murky river water. They can feel the way the electric current spreads through the water.

Fish food

If there is something edible in the water, there is sure to be a fish somewhere that will eat it. There are fish that eat plants, there are fish that eat animals—including other fish—and there are fish that will eat just about anything!

Plankton eaters

Some of the biggest fish in the sea survive by eating some of the smallest living things. Plankton are microscopic plants and animals that drift on ocean currents throughout the world. They are a vital part of an ocean's food chain.

Whale sharks and basking sharks, the biggest fish in the world, live by eating plankton. They have special mouthparts called gill rakers. These filter out the plankton from the water before it passes out through the fish's gills. All bony fish have gill rakers, but fish that eat bigger prey have shorter and more widely spaced gill rakers than the plankton feeders.

BELOW *A basking shark with its mouth open wide sifts tiny sea creatures out of the water as it cruises along.*

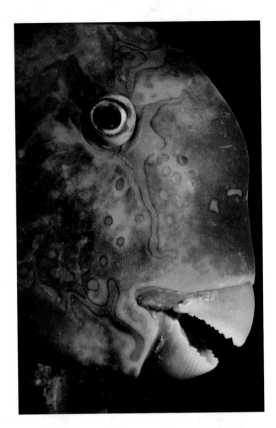

Fish teeth

Many fish eat food that is a lot bigger than plankton. The type of teeth a fish has depends on its diet. Fish can have teeth anywhere in their mouths, not just along the jaw. Some even have teeth on their tongues and inside their throats.

Most fish have simple, cone-shaped teeth to help them hold onto a slippery meal. Some coral reef fish have teeth that are connected to form a single, sharp-edged plate. These fish are well adapted to their diet of hard coral and they can crunch through the shells of oysters, mussels, and other shellfish.

Sharks' teeth

The teeth of a shark are unlike those of any other fish. They are triangular in shape and have razor-sharp edges that can slice through the body of any prey. A shark has several rows of teeth on its powerful jaws, one lying behind the other. Sharks only use the teeth in the front row, but as these become worn or damaged the teeth in the second row take their place. A shark grows new teeth throughout its life.

ABOVE *This parrotfish from Australia's Great Barrier Reef can snip off pieces of coral with its strong jaws.*

RIGHT *A great white shark, one of the ocean's top predators, displays its impressive razor-sharp teeth.*

Jaws

Some fish have jaws that can open very wide to catch their prey. At first glance, the gulper eel that lives in the deep ocean seems to be all mouth. It can swallow animals that are bigger than itself, trapping them in its huge lower jaw, which is similar to a pelican's pouch. Adaptations like this are important for survival on the ocean floor, where food is scarce.

Staying alive

While they are spending time looking for something to eat, most fish have to make sure that they are not about to become food themselves. Fish have a number of ways to escape from predators.

Where's that fish?

One of the best ways to avoid being eaten is by not being seen. Many fish are very well camouflaged. There are fish that look just like strands of seaweed and fish that look like dead leaves. Flatfish, such as the plaice, blend in with the sand and stones of the ocean floor. Some can even change their markings to match their background, making them very hard to see. Ocean-swimming fish, such as mackerel, have a dark-colored back and a silver belly. From above, they blend in with the dark ocean depths, and from below, they are hard to see against the bright sky.

When this leafy sea dragon rests among the seaweed, it will practically vanish from sight.

Don't eat me!

Many fish protect themselves by making themselves difficult to eat. When danger threatens pufferfish and porcupine fish, they suck in water to inflate their bodies, becoming much bigger. This can be enough to startle a predator. Some have spines—which would give the predator another surprise!

Some fish have spines that can deliver a nasty dose of poison. Stonefish, scorpionfish, and zebrafish all have dorsal fin spines that can inject poison. This is a defense against bottom-feeding sharks and rays, but it can also be a painful experience for anyone stepping on one of these fish. A stonefish's spines can go right through a shoe and people have been known to die from its sting.

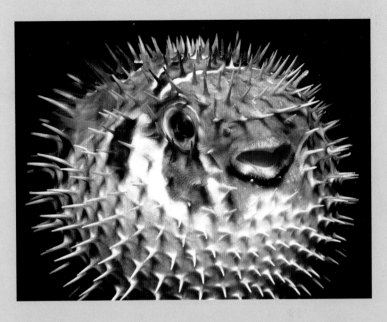

ABOVE *When it feels threatened, the pufferfish blows itself up into a spiky ball to deter attackers.*

These sardines have been herded into a "bait ball" by dolphins to make them easier to eat. Enough will survive to breed the next generation.

Safety in numbers

Some fish survive by staying together. Fish such as herring and minnows gather in big groups called schools. When a predator approaches, the school moves as one to avoid danger. This makes it hard for the predator to pick out a single fish to attack.

Some schools, such as those of damselfish, may even turn on the predator by nipping at it, just as a flock of songbirds might gang up on a hawk. Some predators may even mistake a school for one large fish and avoid attacking altogether.

A new generation

Just about every fish starts life as an egg in the water. Some female fish leave their eggs to float free and unprotected, while others take more care where they place their eggs and they look after them. A few fish, including many sharks, give birth to live young.

Eggs, eggs, eggs

Most of the fish eggs laid in the ocean are very small, perhaps less than 0.04 inches (1 mm) in diameter. In most cases, the male fish fertilizes the eggs after the female has laid them. This egg-laying and fertilizing process is called spawning. Some fish lay huge numbers of eggs. A female herring might produce 50,000 or more in a spawning season, while a female sunfish can lay millions of eggs. Most of these eggs never develop into adult fish, because predators eat most of them.

A male stickleback watches his nest, which is anchored to the streambed by a sticky substance that he produces from his kidneys.

Looking after baby

There are a few stay-at-home fathers in the fish world who take on the job of looking after the eggs. The river-dwelling male stickleback builds a nest using bits of plant material. After the female lays her eggs, the male fertilizes them and then presses them into the safety of the nest. While the eggs develop, he protects them from other fish, including rival sticklebacks, and he fans water over them to make sure they get plenty of oxygen.

Even after the eggs hatch, the male stays around for a few days to look after the young sticklebacks. Male seahorses also take care of the eggs. A male seahorse keeps the eggs safe in a pouch in his belly while they grow.

Is it a boy or a girl?

Some fish can change from being male to being female as they grow older. Some can be male and female at the same time and fertilize their own eggs! The tripod fish, which lives in the deep ocean, is like this. Perhaps this is a useful adaptation that lets the fish overcome the difficulty of finding a mate in the darkness of the deep sea.

Never let me go

Once he finds a female, the tiny male angler fish attaches himself to his much larger mate by his mouth. He remains attached to her for the rest of his life. This means that the female no longer has to search for a male to fertilize her eggs.

BELOW *A tiny male angler fish has attached himself near the larger female's tail. He will spend the rest of his life here.*

Water world

Three-quarters of the surface of the earth is covered by ocean. There are countless miles of rivers and streams, and many ponds and lakes, too.

There is plenty of room on the earth for a fish to find a home—anywhere there is enough clean water to swim in. There are fish in the dark depths of the ocean and in the sun-spotted coral reefs, in the mightiest rivers and in the quietest cave pools. Scientists are discovering new fish every year.

ABOVE *The hairy frogfish, which lives in coral reefs, is one of the fish world's more unusual members.*

WOW!

The world's deepest-living fish was found in an ocean trench more than 27,000 feet (8,200 m) deep . Scientists know very little about how this mysterious creature lives.

Fish features

It is difficult to describe what a fish is, although most share some common features. All fish live in water and breathe through gills, but a few, such as mudskippers, can survive for a short time on land. Fish have fins to propel them through the water. Only fish have swim bladders, but not all fish have them. All but the jawless fish have scales. Most fish lay eggs, but a few give birth to live young.

Endangered fish

Fish have adapted to life in the water in as many complex and fascinating ways as other animals have adapted to a life on land. Their water world is a very different place from the world we air-breathers live in. Even after all the centuries that humans have spent traveling and exploring the world's oceans, there is still a great deal we do not know about the realm beneath the waves.

WOW!

In 2005, sharks killed four people. On the other hand, we eat more than 110 million tons (100 million t) of fish every year, including sharks.

Living underwater doesn't protect fish from the activities of humans. They are still hunted, and their habitats are threatened. Overfishing has reduced the numbers of many kinds of fish. Freshwater fish are threatened by the pollution of rivers and by humans using water for their own needs. To prevent fish from disappearing, we must learn to share the world's water with them and eat fewer fish so their populations have a chance to grow again.

ABOVE *Overfishing means that schools of fish such as these herring are becoming increasingly rare.*

Glossary

Adaptation   A feature of a living thing that makes it better suited to its particular lifestyle; the ability to get oxygen from the water through their gills is an adaptation of fish.

Barbels   Long feelers that some fish have around their mouths. Barbels can detect tastes and smells and are used to find food in murky places such as muddy river bottoms.

Bony fish   The largest of the three main groups of fish—there are more bony fish than any other kind. Bony fish have skeletons made of bone.

Buoyancy   The ability of an object to stay afloat in the water.

Camouflage   Colors or patterns on a fish or other animal that make it hard to see against its surroundings.

Capsule   A protective container for something.

Cartilage   A tough, flexible material that makes up the skeletons of some fish, such as sharks. It is also found in the joints of other animals, including humans.

Eardrum   The part of the human ear that picks up sound vibrations traveling through the air. Fish don't have eardrums.

Fertilize   To make an egg fertile—the male fish has to fertilize the female's eggs before new fish can develop inside the egg.

Fins   The parts that a fish uses to move itself through the water: the anal fin is the belly fin, used for balance; the caudal fin is the tail fin, used for propulsion; the dorsal fin is the back fin, used for balance; the pectoral and pelvic fins are the paired fins on either side of the body, used for steering.

Food chain   The relationship between living things that shows who gets eaten by whom.

Gills   Parts of a fish's body that it uses to take oxygen from the water. Gills do the same job that lungs do for air-breathing animals.

Gill filaments   The delicate, folded parts of the gills where oxygen is absorbed from the water.

Gill flap   The hard, outer covering that protects the gills.

Gill rakers   Parts of the gills that trap any debris from the water before it passes over the delicate, oxygen-absorbing gill filaments.

Jawless fish   One of the three main groups of fish; they have no jaws, no scales, smooth skin and skeletons made of cartilage.

Lateral line   A system of detectors along the side of a fish that senses movements and vibrations in the water; some amphibians also have lateral line detectors.

Lens   Part of the eye that focuses the light coming through it.

Plankton   Tiny plants and animals, too small to be seen without a microscope, that drift in the ocean currents.

Retina   Part of the eye that detects light coming into it.

School   A large group of fish of the same kind swimming together. A group of fish can also be called a shoal.

Skeleton   The structure of bone or cartilage inside an animal that strengthens the body and protects the soft parts inside; it also provides anchor points for the animal's muscles.

Spawning   The time when female fish release their eggs.

Streamlined   Shaped to cut smoothly through the water with as little resistance as possible.

Swim bladder   The part of the body that fish use to change their depth in the water. They do this by adjusting the amount of gas in the swim bladder.

Taste buds   Tiny parts of the body used to detect tastes. Most land animals, including humans, have taste buds on the upper surface of the tongue, but fish can have them all over their bodies.

Web sites

www.marinebiology.org/fish.htm
An overview of ichthyology—what scientists call the study of fish.

www.seasky.org/sea.html
Web site with a lot of fun information on fish, other inhabitants of the sea, and on ocean exploration.

www.fishonline.org/
Information from the Marine Conservation Society about declining fish populations, including which fish to eat and which to avoid.

http://dsc.discovery.com/convergence/blueplanet/sounds/sounds.html
Hear for yourself the sounds made by some noisy fish and other sea creatures.

www.nature.org/joinanddonate/rescuereef/explore/video.html
Watch video clips of life beneath the sea in coral reefs around the world.

Index